CABELL UNDER FIRE

CABELL UNDER FIRE

FOUR ESSAYS
by
GEOFFREY MORLEY-MOWER

THE JAMES BRANCH CABELL SERIES

REVISIONIST PRESS
New York   1975

Library of Congress Cataloging in Publication Data

Morley-Mower, Geoffrey.
  Cabell under fire : four essays.

  CONTENTS: Jurgen and the reputation of James Branch Cabell.--James Branch Cabell's flirtation with Clio.--Sinclair Lewis and his attempts to reform James Branch Cabell.--Cabell under fire.
  1. Cabell, James Branch, 1879-1958--Addresses, essays, lectures. I. Title.
PS3505.A153Z72   813'.5'2   74-31094
ISBN 0-87700-214-2

Copyright © 1975 by Geoffrey Morley-Mower
All rights reserved.

This edition is limited to 200 copies.

THE REVISIONIST PRESS
G.P.O. Box 2009
Brooklyn, N. Y. 11202

Printed and Bound in the United States of America

TABLE OF CONTENTS

Jurgen and the Reputation of James Branch Cabell 5

James Branch Cabell's Flirtation with Clio 11

Sinclair Lewis and his Attempts to Reform
    James Branch Cabell 20

Cabell Under Fire 24

AUTHOR'S NOTE

It is close to a crime to treat Cabell solemnly, for he, of all recent satirists of the human condition, is the least solemn. I have tried in these pieces not to be too dull about an author whose chief gift was a sense of humour, exercised so many times on pompous critics. Yet Cabell, of course, did have his serious side, and perhaps he would not be gaining so much critical attention today if it were not so. Confronted by the modern doubt regarding the existence of God, he refused to panic, like Carlyle, into inventing some sort of tolerable substitute. What he did was to carry out a good-humoured investigation of the matter. He made enormous fun of the more anthropomorphic imaginations of mankind, but his scepticism was limited by the fact that he seems to have been a genuinely happy man. The protagonists he invented that were the closest to his own condition loved their wives and were mystified by the extraordinary generosity meeted out to them — by life, by Koschei, by God, by the blind fates. His last alter ego, Smirt, warns the heavens against trying to bully him by remarking that he will not be "convinced by a thunderbolt and that any such display of brute force would but lay you open to a charge of peevishness." But he goes on to give thanks for the beauty of the world and to describe himself finally as a "Peripatetic Episcopalian" following a "discreet path between piety and atheism." He is jesting, of course, as always, but the piety is real and irreducible. To my mind the dialogue between Cabell's piety and Cabell's atheism is the most interesting thing about this most orginal literary artist.

When I was a schoolboy in London in the Thirties, Cabell was the author everybody was reading and talking about. I remember thinking that *Chivalry* was the most beautiful book I had ever read and that *Jurgen* was the cleverest. We thrilled to the veiled obscenities and rallied to his attack on puritanical Christianity, from which most of us had suffered in one way or another. What we failed to see was that Cabell had no vested interest in immorality and was satirizing, more than anything else, the human tendency to form narrow-minded, embattled orthodoxies that could not be justified at the court of reason. He had never decided himself between piety and atheism and the strength of his position, paradoxically, was precisely because he sat on the fence. He did not pretend to be comfortable there and he made much of the foolishness of his own posture—a little less foolish, however, than the committed zealots on either side.

The essays in this volume have little unity of theme, but the reader may note a harping on Cabell's Southern-ness. It is because Cabell was a Southerner that he took such pleasure in pouring scorn on the spurious achievements of a commercial society that had had no mercy on his own people. Because he was a Southerner of the old stock, his sense of his own identity could stand the strain of disagreeing with everyone about everything. His treatment of the sacred cows of North and South lost him readers on both sides of the Mason-Dixon Line. He never conformed his work to public expectations and his intelligence never failed coolly to criticize his emotions. He remains one of the minor delights of our era and his unique method of remaining sane in a mad world can be applied as well in 1974 as when he sat down to write his books in Richmond-in-Virginia.

Acknowledgements are made to Mrs. James Branch Cabell, who gave permission for all quotations from her husband's books and private letters. Acknowledgements are also made to *KALKI*, Studies in James Branch Cabell, published by the University of Cincinnati, which first published "Jurgen and the Reputation of James Branch Cabell," and The Yale University Library Gazette, which first published "James Branch Cabell's Flirtation with Clio: The Story of a Collaboration."

Harrisonburg, Virginia
May 1974

JURGEN AND THE REPUTATION OF
JAMES BRANCH CABELL

James Branch Cabell is not only an undeservedly neglected author, he is a widely misunderstood one. Edmund Wilson, among others, has protested against the neglect but has done nothing to clear up the misunderstanding which has often represented Cabell as an atheist, a blasphemer, and a pornographer.[1] The importance of setting straight the record is perhaps now greater than it has ever been, for there are signs of a Cabell revival on the way.

In judging whether the revival of interest in Cabell is likely to be of any magnitude, the first question to consider might well be to what extent his neglect was brought about by external circumstances and how much can be attributed to defects in the works themselves. Wilson points to Cabell's occasionally precious and archaic diction and most critics would agree that many of his idiosyncracies are indefensible— for example, his habit of writing "not ever" rather than "never" and "a little by a little" instead of the more familiar usage. The faults, however, are outweighed by a multitude of virtues, and it is unlikely that a small amount of bad writing among a great deal of good could be responsible for his neglect. Since the late twenties, when his work went out of fashion, the intellectual and moral climate of the English-speaking world has been hostile, not only to his message—which can be summed up as a civilized hesitancy before the existential realities—but also to the detached tone of his writing. At a period when the nations were being called to arms and, after 1945, held in a permanent crisis, the quiet and quizzical voice seemed inappropriate, the style merely mannered, the subject matter remote.

During the last decade, however, there have been changes in popular taste, favouring the fantastic and the philosophical, which could make Cabell of interest once again. J. R. Tolkien has become, through his books on the Hobbits, a race of little people living in the dawn of history, something of a cult figure for the young people both in Britain and America, and his books are to be seen in paperbacks in drug stores. There are sound reasons for Tolkien's popularity. The conflict between the western democracies and the Communist bloc has found its literary equivalent in Tolkien's war between the good Hobbits and the evil goblins and it is not surprising that his vogue has been more marked in America, where the burden of opposing Communist expansion is most felt and where the tendency to reduce complex political struggles to clear moral issues is most pronounced. However, the climate of opinion continues to change, no doubt due to the long duration of the Viet-Nam war. Among the youth we now have disillusionment with political parties, anti-war sentiment and a cynical attitude towards materialist values. Cabell has all of this, and in the past it has prejudiced readers against him. It may dispose them to him in the future.

Moreover, if allegorical works featuring imaginary kingdoms are in fashion again, Cabell, whom Edmund Wilson has compared to Flaubert and Swift, is Tolkien's literary superior and has a more complex product to purvey. "If we must read about imaginary kingdoms," Wilson writes, "give me James Branch Cabell. He at least wrote for grown-up people and he does not present the drama of life as a showdown between good people and goblins. He can cover more ground in an episode that lasts only three pages than Tolkien is able to in one of his twenty-page chapters and he can create a more disquieting impression by reference to something that is never described than Tolkien through his whole demonology."[2]

Beginning with *Jurgen* in 1919, we come to what many critics consider his mature work. It was followed by the three books which have received most critical acclaim — *The High Place* (1923), *The Silver Stallion* (1926), and *Something About Eve* (1927). He went on to write other books over the next twenty-five years, but it is probably that posterity will consider the books mentioned above his major achievements.

Jurgen was his first book to be an outstanding commercial success and it is the first one of his books to have been printed in paperback. There is, however, a reluctance among critics to judge it is his best book. Arvin Wells[3] and Joe Lee Davis,[4] both of whom have produced full length studies, are tentative in their value judgements on individual books. Wilson prefers *The High Place to Jurgen.*[5] Cabell himself objected to those who compared his other works unfavourably with *Jurgen* and insisted that all the 'Poictesme' books were chapters of one book and that the public "should select whatsoever chapter it may please them as the least inadequate chapter of my large book." Against such solid opposition it may be presumptuous to assert the superiority of *Jurgen*, but Cabell himself, while he was writing the book, certainly realized that something in the story had released an unaccustomed flood of creative energy.

He began it as a short story, but it soon wriggled out of its creator's grasp and demanded fuller treatment. Writing excitedly from Richmond, he announced to his friend Burton Rascoe that he intended "to make of this thing a book of noble and majestic proportions, though it involves the squandering of every idea I possess."[6] This was prophetic because *Jurgen* seems to express his central themes — particularly his ideas on the nature of reality and the distortions of the romantic termperament — with greater clarity than in his other works. Moreover, the density of ironic incident, satire, humor, and passages of poetic prose is greater than he achieved elsewhere. The suppression of the book on a charge of pornography was in one respect fortunate in that it brought the book readers and cleared the ground for other writers who were similarly hemmed in by the prudish standards of the censors. In another respect it was unfortunate, for Cabell got the reputation of being a "pornographic" writer and lost many readers who might have sustained his reputation beyond the twenties.

Jurgen, whether or not it is Cabell's best book, is certainly one of his most typical and it contains all those features for which the author has been so liberally criticized. It begins with the central character, an ageing pawnbroker, who is also a poet, passing the Cistercian Abbey on his way home from his shop. He meets a monk, who has just stubbed his toe on a stone and is cursing the devil, and Jurgen ventures an elaborate and poetic defense of his Satanic majesty. He passes on and is approaching his home when he meets a black gentleman who thanks him for his good word. In conversation, Jurgen lets it out that his wife does not "quite understand him." When he reaches his home his wife is not found anywhere and, suspecting that it is the Price of Darkness who has removed her, he resolves to "do the manly thing" and retrieve her. She has been seen by neighbors acting strangely near a cave outside the town, so, with some trepidation, Jurgen approaches the cave and enters.[7]

Now the black gentleman is not Satan but a far more exalted figure, none other than Koschei the Deathless, who made things as they are, the Creator and Manager of the Universe, who obligingly dispatches Jurgen on a year-long romp, equipped with the loan of his youthful body in search of "justice" — which can be interpreted as a search for a meaning in life. The allegory is complicated, because while Jurgen ostensibly is searching for his crosspatch of a spouse he actually is seeking his fulfillment in one woman after another. Underneath the picaresque incident and the mountebankery of the central character it is an investigation of the nature of reality and how, in the light of modern knowledge, a man of the western tradition should deal with the truths and untruths of religion, history, politics and popular philosophy.

Traveling through various mythological realms, he possesses Guinevere before her marriage to Arthur, lives with a nature goddess in Cocaigne, with a hamadryad in ancient Greece and with a vampire in hell. In spite of the farcical treatment of Jurgen's lovemaking he is, in these episodes, testing, in the most amusing and delicate way, various conventional systems of thought that have at one time or another captured the imagination of men.

Satirical elements abound. Hell is a democracy and Satan has been elected president and voted extraordinary powers for the duration of the war with heaven. There is a peace party and a vociferous war party bristling with infernal patriotism. Jurgen, whose nature it is to compromise with the Mammon of iniquity, particularly when his tenure is not sound, makes a long speech in council, satirizing a certain type of democratic politician who wishes to impose the utmost rigors of the law on all those whose patriotism is doubtful. It is a criticism of McCarthy before McCarthy — but performed in mock-medieval manner, with much display of invented authorities. Heaven is protected by a roof, lowered during wartime on earth to prevent the celestial ears from being offended by the blasphemous prayers for victory of the contending nations.

After ascending the throne of Almighty God but feeling uncomfortable there, Jurgen terminates his researches by returning to Amneran Heath, entering the cave there and asking Koschei for his old wife back again.

The central message of the book is that Jurgen — who stands allegorically for mankind, questing for satisfaction of its dreams and desires — finds no where what he is looking for. And, not in despair, but in a sort of humourous acceptance, he returns gratefully to the routine pieties and exasperations of ordinary existence. On one level it is a frustrated sortie of the human spirit. On another level it is an affirmation of religious values, for Jurgen rejects the nihilistic conclusion to his adventure. In a passage remarkable for its humour as well as for the disquieting atmosphere to which Edmund Wilson has alluded — nihilism is tested and found wanting. The Brown man with queer feet (who is Pan), takes Jurgen into the darkness of a wood and there shows him "all." He exits from this experience shaken but defiantly argumentative.

"Slay me, then!" says Jurgen with shut eyes, for he did not at all like the appearance of things. ". . . but it is beyond your power to make me believe that there is no justice anywhere or that I am unimportant . . . I am fettered by cowardice, I am enfeebled by disastrous memories; and I am maimed by old follies. Still, I seem to detect in myself something which is permanent and rather fine. Underneath everything, and in spite of everything, I really do seem to detect that something. What role that something is to enact after the death of my body, and upon what stage I cannot guess. When fortune knocks I shall open the door. Meanwhile I tell you candidly, you brown man, there is something in Jurgen far too admirable for any intelligent arbiter ever to fling into the dustheap . . . I believe I can contrive some trick to cheat oblivion when the need arises," says Jurgen, trembling, but, even so, with his mind quite made up about it.[8]

This does not place Cabell in the front rank of pious fideists, but it is a positive enough statement of belief in man's significance, which is at least the necessary basis for a religious attitude to life. It is not, moreover, contradicted by his more explicitly philosophical non-fiction works. In *Beyond Life* he defines man as "an ape, reft of his tail and grown rusty at climbing who yet . . . feels himself to be a symbol and a frail representative of omnipotence in a place that is not home.[9] Once again the philosophical statement is more poetical than philosophical and we may well ask where Cabell stands; but we will not get a clear answer from him, for he revels in the lack of clarity in his position and that of his various protagonists. His platform, if we may put it that way, is deliberately equivocal. What we do know is that he was not an unqualified sceptic and that he commonly attended divine service at the Episcopal Church in Richmond. This does not locate the exact religious position of our luminary, but he shines nevertheless, however dubiously.

Arvin Wells has suggested that Cabell belonged to a group of thinkers, including Bertrand Russell, Unamuno, Hans Vaehinger and Santayana, who, while regretting the fact that Christianity was no longer believable, felt that it was necessary to go on behaving "as if" the moral universe of Christian ideals still existed.[10] I do not wish to claim philosophical originality for Cabell — it is sufficient to claim his imaginative originality — but it can be argued that he parted significantly from that group, in the direction of orthodox belief.

His criticism of Christianity is confined, for one thing, to its anthropomorphic manifestations. In *Quiet Please*, one of his latter books of reminiscences, he recalls that when he was young he always thought of God as "an elderly Jewish gentleman, addicted to wearing dressing gowns, who after the

Crucifixion had joined the Catholic Church, and later had become an Episcopalian."[11]
This comment is on a level with the satire on the "Heaven of Jurgen's Grandmother" and the imaginative version of hell conjured up by Coth of the Rocks; that is, it is not barbed with theological distaste, it is modified by humour and it makes fair comment on the history of Christianity. For example, in the interview with the Almighty God, who appears conventionally in a white beard, Jurgen protests no very strong faith in divinity but adds "you were loved by those whom I greatly loved a long while ago and it seems to me that dates and manuscripts and the opinion of learned persons are very trifling things besides what I remember and what I envy." And God says — brilliantly preserving the balance of the irony and the opacity of the central philosophy — "who could have expected such a monstrous clever fellow as you Jurgen ever to have envied the illusions of an old woman?"[12]

If Cabell can be defended against the charges of atheism and blasphemy, he can even more easily be acquitted of writing pornography, though this last accusation has been the most persistent. When *Jurgen* first appeared his publishers were indicted before the Grand Jury of the County of New York for intending to "sell and show a lewd, lascivious, indecent, obscure and disgusting book entitled *Jurgen*, a more particular description of which said book would be offensive to this Court and improper to spread upon the records thereof, wherefore such description is not here given."[13] Commenting to Guy Holt January 17, 1920, Cabell protests that he "cannot find a sentence in the book that could not be read aloud in Sunday School."[14] This is perhaps to exaggerate his innocence but it can be doubted if his oblique and sophisticated treatment of sexual themes ever did have the force of phornography. They certainly do not today.

When Jurgen and Anaitis come to the high grey walls of Cocaigne, the following conversation takes place:

"You must knock two or three times," says Anaitis, "to get into Cocaigne." Jurgen observed the bronze knocker upon the door, and he grinned in order to hide his embarrassment. "It is a quaint fancy," said he, "and the two constituents of it appear to have been modelled from life." "They were copied very exactly from Adam and Eve," says Anaitis, "who were the first persons to open this gateway." "Why then," says Jurgen, "There is no earthly doubt that men degenerate, since here under my hand is the proof of it." With that he knocked, and the door opened and the two of them entered."[15]

The passage can, of course, be justified by its wit and its appropriateness to the realm of bodily pleasure. But the whole point of the Cocaigne episode is not to celebrate sensuality but to eliminate an exclusively sexual solution to the problems of human existence. This strictly moral tale would work equally well if applied to what has been called the Playboy philosophy or the modern drug scene. What Cabell is saying is that it is boring to become involved in the endless liturgies of sex (or drugs), but it is amusing enough to read about it.

In his non-fiction works he continually complained of his unjustified repuration for lewdness and of his uncomprehending admirers, "the hordes of idiots and prurient fools and busybodies, of unpublished authors, well worthy of that condition, of dabblers in black magic, of catamites and of amateur strumpets."[16]

Cabell explicitly answers the New York Censors in the court scene in Philistia, when Jurgen is tried for lewdness. His accuser, an insect, demands his relegation to Limbo, "for he is offensive and lewd and lascivious and indecent" — the very words of the censor's indictment. The grounds of the charge are that Jurgen went through a sort of marriage ceremony with Queen Anaitis in Cocaigne in which Jurgen carried a raised lance and broke with it a sacred veil. The symbolism is sexual but the passage is not pornographic, for Cabell describes nothing specific and the erotic imagination of the reader has nothing to hold on to. Jurgen, in his defense, replies that "these pages bear a sword and a lance and a staff, and nothing else whatever; and you deduce, I hope, that all the lewdness is in the insectival mind of him who itches to be calling these things by other names."[17] If the rather obvious joke can be forgiven, whereby the pages of Cabell's novel are also the pages of the court of Philistia who are holding the offensive weapons, the argument for the defense may seem cogent. Unfortunately mud sticks and no amount of argufying seems to remove it.

Carl Van Doren makes a contrast between Melville and Cabell, both so dominated in their different ways by a reaction to the Puritan code. But Cabell's wit, says Van Doren, is not so inhibited by religion as Melville's and plays "with conscience and immorality and blasphemy" (he might have added sexuality) without fear and "good humouredly strokes the beard of Jehovah."[18] It is not my intention to draw literary parallels but simply to note that Melville was accused of unorthodoxy and nameless moral faults, and his books died in his own lifetime only to be resurrected after his death. Cabell suffered a similar fate but the reasons for his eclipse of reputation are not so personal and much can be attributed to the drowning out of his singular, sly voice by the noise of international conflict. But unlike Melville, his literary reputation has not yet been restored, and a movement to bring him once more before a wide public is only beginning.

The best hope for such a restoration must lie in his relevance to youth. Cabell was brought up in the aftermath of the Civil War in a ruined South. His sense of outrage as a Southerner at the injustices of history and his feeling for the helplessness of the sentient individual against the "big fists" of the powerful makes him, in a strange way, a contemporary to the college student today, threatened by nuclear war and uncertain of the already fading promises of a materialistic future. The problem is that Cabell will not be put before students while a slightly uncomfortable smirk appears on middle-aged faces at the mention of his name. The students themselves, looking for pornography in Cabell, will not find it and it can be doubted if an independent taste for fine writing will lead them to him. Yet Cabell's fiction—and particularly JURGEN—would not only be good for their education in letters, but— to use an old-fashioned expression—it would also be good for their souls. Because the diseases of youth are vague idealism and sensual escapism, it could only be beneficial to young people to connect with a mind that has thought such attitudes through to their conclusions and deftly charted a way ahead. Faith in the eternal verities is an essential element in the progress of civilization, but scepticism is an equally essential disinfector of false values. The PLAYBOY solutions to life need to be laughed out of court, and no one is better equipped to laugh them out than Cabell.

NOTES

[1] Edmund Wilson, "The James Branch Cabell Case Reopened," *The Bit Between My Teeth*, New York: Farrar, Straus & Giroux, 1965.
[2] Edmund Wilson, "O, O Those Awful Orcs!" *The Bit Between My Teeth*, p. 332.
[3] Arvin R. Wells, *Jesting Moses*, University of Florida Press, 1962.
[4] Joe Lee Davis, *James Branch Cabell*, New York, Twaine Publishing Inc., 1962.
[5] Edmund Wilson, "The James Branch Cabell Case Reopened," *The Bit Between My Teeth*, p. 313.
[6] Padraic Colum (edit), *Between Friends*, New York, Harcourt, Brace & World, 1962, p. 84.
[7] James Branch Cabell, *Jurgen*, New York, Robert McBride & Co., 1927, p. 13.
[8] *Jurgen*, p. 125-126.
[9] James Branch Cabell, *Beyond Life*, New York, Robert McBride & Co., 1927, p. 201.
[10] Wells, *Jesting Moses*, p. 13.
[11] James Branch Cabell, *Quiet Please*, University of Florida Press, 1952, p. 41.
[12] Cabell, *Jurgen*, p. 305.
[13] *Between Friends*, p. 157.
[14] *Between Friends*, p. 158.
[15] Cabell, *Jurgen*, p. 146.
[16] James Branch Cabell, *As I Remember It*, New York, The McBride Co., 1955, p. 238.
[17] Cabell, *Jurgen*, p. 239.
[18] Carl Van Doren, *James Branch Cabell*, New York, Robert McBride & Co., 1928, p. 85.

JAMES BRANCH CABELL'S FLIRTATION WITH CLIO: THE STORY OF A COLLABORATION

In the Collection of American Literature in the Beinecke Library are some 154 letters and four telegrams from James Branch Cabell to A. J. Hanna, the historian who collaborated with him on a book in the "Rivers of America" series, *The St. Johns*.[1] With the letters (which were purchased in 1965 on Alvord and American Studies funds) are copies of 33 letters and two telegrams from Hanna to Cabell. The correspondence spans the years 1938 to 1954, but most of it grew out of the active collaboration on *The St. Johns,* 1940 to 1943. In the Alderman Library at the University of Virginia the first, second, and final typed drafts of the book can be seen. Hanna's type is large, Cabell's small, and the handwriting of the two men also can be differentiated in the various drafts. The letters reveal Cabell as a consistently witty correspondent, conscious of his own special gifts as a creative artist and devoted to exercising those gifts at whatever grief to himself, his collaborator—and even the Muse of History.

Before 1930 James Branch Cabell's output had been mainly fiction. He had published—apart from his purely genealogical works—only two non-fictional books, *Beyond Life* (1919) and *Straws and Prayer Books* (1924), designed respectively as the prologue and the epilogue to what he called "The Biography of the Life of Manuel," that "large book" of which each of his novels was to be an episode. But in the 1930s, with the popularity of his fiction in decline, he at first turned out a series of books which combined fictional elements with essay material and then finally took up historical themes in earnest.

In 1942 he published *The First Gentleman of America,* a fictional treatment of a historical character, Nemattonon, an Indian prince who traveled to Mexico and Spain, becoming a Christian and taking the name of Don Luis de Velasco. The story is one tailored to Cabell's ironical view of life, for Don Luis, westernized on the surface, turns away from the white man at the end and, after leading his people in a slaughter of Spaniards, disappears forever. Cabell tells the story, however, as if it were folklore presented by a scholar and provides his hero with fictional love affairs and an attitude of gallantry appropriate to a protagonist in "The Biography."

The researches necessary for the writing of *The First Gentleman* brought Cabell to St. Augustine, and it was there, in January 1941, that he met Stephen Vincent Benet. Benet was at this time, with Carl Carmer, editing the "Rivers of America" series for Farrar and Rinehart, and Cabell asked him who was to do the St. Johns River on which St. Augustine stood. When Benet suggested that Cabell should undertake it himself, he pleaded insufficient historical background; but Benet countered by saying that "your friend, Professor Hanna, to whom you dedicated *The First Gentleman,* knows all about Florida's history . . . it is Hanna's specialty."[2]

A. J. Hanna was then a professor of history at Rollins College, not far from St. Augustine. He had struck up a friendship with Cabell some years previously and more recently, while Cabell was writing *The First Gentleman,* had been assisting him with a book list on the Menendez period of Florida's history. Nothing could have been more natural than that these two friends, already unofficial collaborators, should join forces to write a history of the St. Johns River. Cabell, sixty at the time, and with his major work behind him, was pleased at the idea that he could "round off the catalogue of my writings by including among them a book of history."[3]

Cabell's idea of history, however, was not entirely orthodox. He was a great admirer of Gibbon and relished the notion of writing an ironical commentary on the American past that would express his own philosophical point of view and also be good literature. But for nearly thirty years he had been pouring out novels about the imaginary medieval realm of Poictesme, in which he had been completely in command of his own puppet show. In this fantasy universe he had confidently created whole mythologies and had decorated his works with an apparatus of invented scholarship which runs through them with the insistence of a stock joke. However, confronted with the task of writing genuine history, he seems not to have hesitated before accepting the challenge.

The story of the writing of this book is largely that of Cabell's cheerful but implacable determination to impose his own pattern on history, rather than sit down humbly before the facts. The massive but not ignoble egotism that enabled him to write his thirty-four books, maintaining his own high standards regardless of the adulation or disapproval of the general public—a quality which Edmund Wilson mentions with admiration—was to be clearly demonstrated in the making of *The St. Johns.*[4] In a letter to Hanna, dated 29 February 1940, Cabell made the point at the outset: " . . . I am not setting up," he wrote, "as a 'sober-sided historian,' at my age, and I still mean to touch history, if at all, with a free hand." But in his letter of 4 May 1941, he wrote disarmingly:

> *My conscience boggles at the fact, so far as I can see, you will have to write the book, and I trim it with a few fripperies of rhetoric; . . . It sounds like an unfair arrangement for you, but in the end we would both get out of the book, I believe, an assured amount of kudos as well as some possible cash.*

The scheme was for Hanna to produce a draft of each chapter which Cabell would then re-write or touch up in his own personal style. The published book shows little evidence of patching through variations in style and the casual reader may be forgiven for assuming that Cabell wrote the entire work in his own ironic vein based on raw facts produced by Hanna. But as the drafts show, this is very far from the truth. Neither author was a lay figure and both contributed in full measure to the finished work. It is a happy coincidence that Hanna's sense of humor and attitude to the vagaries of human history were as deeply ironical as Cabell's. There was something of the novelist in the historian and—as we shall see—something of the historian in the novelist. The result was a book that had, as its unifying note, a detached good humor that came from both authors in equal measure.

As an example, here is Hanna's account of an incident which in style and tone of mockery might have been written by Cabell:

> *Having uttered these inspiring words, Menendez knelt, and he entreated a continuance of Heaven's charity, before leading his men into the woods south of the fort. His prayers were answered, at once, with a benignant generosity, since in these woods they found thirty-eight naked Frenchmen, whom the Spaniards shot down, laughingly and at leisure, with the French guns. It was excellent, said the Spaniards, to wind up a hard day's work with this half hour of sportsmanship.*[5]

It is clear from this passage that Cabell was at no time imposing his own special point of view on Hanna's text. Both men were highly literate Southerners of the "old stock" and their humorous, postbellum bitterness was bred in the bone. As far as the collaboration was concerned, this was a highly favorable factor.

Before work had been started, however, Cabell's concept of the book began to dominate. On 22 November 1941 he wrote Hanna that Benet wanted "the picturesque rather than the merely instructive associations of our river." Later (30 January 1942) he elaborated on this idea, which seems to reflect his own views more certainly than Benet's, by saying that he had begun "to form a few notions as to revising it (the St. Johns material) in a style combining the more happy features of Gibbon and Guedalla. You have to supply the facts.—Which reminds me to ask if Menendez landed with six ships, as you declare."

Cabell was far from content, as it turned out, to be a mere embellisher of another man's material. He had a genuine interest in history for its own sake and had read deeply in the Menendez period for the writing of *The First Gentleman.* He had even made a remarkable discovery. In 1940, while rummaging in the junk room of the City Hall in St. Augustine, he had come across the coffin of this Don Pedro Menendez, the founder of the city, who had died in 1574. The bones had been removed in 1924 and reinterred in the Cathedral of Aviles; the headboard had been taken to Stetson University, but the coffin had been abandoned in the junk room.[6] Cabell was forever probing for facts and was obviously delighted by the raw material of history, but his desire to make mocking comments on human folly was greater than Hanna's and many of his amendments to Hanna's drafts involve a refining of the irony.

He was always aware of the necessity to make the book amusing and, if possible, better than any other book in the series. He enjoyed the collaboration and never let up on his friend. On 29 March 1942 he wrote:

> ... I struck a little fresh trouble in the Hawkins episode. He had four ships, not three; and it was not he who wrote the account of his second voyage, but a man named John Sparke.

A few days later (4 April 1942) he gleefully challenged Hanna:

> Now then! In the teeth of both you historians (Hanna and his wife were both history scholars who had written books) I hurl the fact that Hawkins was not knighted until 1588. And, I ask, far more humbly, just when was Menendez imprisoned?

There follows, in the same letter, an example of his cajoling style and his method of getting the kind of facts he wanted:

> For the next three chapters I have, I believe, enough material in hand. I would like, though, some special detail as to Denys Rolle, such as whether (Like James Grant) he was partial to rattlesnake meat, or (like Governor Oglethorpe) may have been a younger brother to the Old Pretender. And then, too, is not anything known about Henry Woodward? I want, in brief, the definite, the unique.

Cabell, in fact, was after the scandalous and had been well pleased at Hanna's draft account of the philanthropical and military activities of James Oglethorpe, who brought seven hundred jailbirds, imprisoned for debt in the Fleet and elsewhere, to Georgia as laborers under the mistaken impression that the silkworm could be cultivated there.

Evidence that Cabell was active in his own research and was not simply being fed facts by Hanna abounds in the letters. He chided Hanna good humoredly (22 June 1942) for missing the comedy of the conflict between James Grant, the eccentric governor of East Florida, and the even more eccentric Denys Rolle, who established a colony of reformed prostitutes on the banks of the St. Johns:

> You astound me by missing the comedy of their deep-seated and yet superficially polite six-year-long conflict. I can but thank God and Marchman (of the Florida Historical Association) for a sight of Grant's two letters about Denys Rolle.

He was concerned with making the historical events immediate and the narrative lively. "You will note," he had written on 16 June 1942, "how I am beginning to bring in dialogue. It lightens the text so nicely." It may be imagined that Hanna was not necessarily pleased with the idea. The dialogue is witty, and ironical points are constantly made, but it is all in Cabell's voice, which does not add to the atmosphere of historical accuracy which the historian must have longed for. But Cabell was amply justified in his pursuit of interesting eccentrics.

In one of the passages written entirely by Cabell and not based on a first draft by Hanna, the tracing of the career of Daniel McGirth, who deserted from the American Army and afterward served the British as a Lieutenant Colonel of the East Florida Rangers (and after whom McGirth's Creek was named) brings the whole Revolutionary period of history alive. McGirth, after the

English departed, turned to the Indians and plundered Americans and Spaniards indiscriminately. He was finally captured by the Spaniards and walled up in an underground cell of the Castillado de San Marcos where, five years later, he died. Cabell turns novelist to describe the dreary end to an adventurous life.[7]

The McGirth episode was one that Benet liked especially when he saw the first draft of the book. In a letter to John Farrar, on 1 October 1942, he described the text as "too lush" and complained of its going "out of gear" at times:

> *When it is meshing, of course, it is fine—the death of McGirth, the Menendez-Ribaut stuff, the character of William Bartram, the little scene of Jefferson drinking his amontillado. But, somehow or other, there's a lot that should be simpler . . . I realize this is the first draft.*

It is interesting to note here that the death of McGirth was written by Cabell, the Menendez-Ribaut "stuff" largely by Hanna, and the chapter on William Bartram was a joint effort with Cabell re-writing as a novelist what Hanna had set down more straightforwardly. Mr. Jefferson, drinking his amontillado after the purchase of Florida from Spain for five million dollars, was Cabell's inspiration, though in his first draft the amontillado appeared as "a discreet toddy."

Cabell was, as usual, good-humored about Benet's strictures, and the work went on. *The St. Johns* was going to be like no other book in the series, if Cabell had anything to do with it, and it was going to scandalize a number of people. That was made clear by Benet in the letter to Farrar already quoted:

> *As a guidebook, I should say it would annoy impartially Catholics, Protestants, Friends, as well as persons of British, Spanish or French descent and admirers of democracy, the British empire, and republican institutions. I cannot see it clasped to the breast of the tourist. However it ought to stir up any number of hornet's nests and that often aids in sales.*

The necessity of making the book lively and interesting was everpresent to Cabell and—evidently on the occasion of their meeting to discuss progress in June 1942—he had promised Hanna to write something on the Richmond of Edgar Allan Poe. ". . . the job proved," he reported on 8 July 1942, "t be intricate; in fact, if published, it may get me lynched in Virginia . . ." No mention of Poe appears in the final version or in any of the drafts, but it may be doubted whether Cabell would have flinched from publication because of unpopularity in his native place. It is far more likely that the piece was dropped because it had little relevance to the history of the St. Johns.

Cabell wrote his severest letter to Hanna on 13 August 1942, about the unpleasantness that had developed because Hanna, in good faith, had handed the draft of the chapter on the early Quakers to Professor Charles M. Andrews, a colleague with a specialty in that field. Andrews apparently wrote angrily to Cabell to protest both treatment and accuracy. Cabell's tolerant and amused attitude toward the trials and tribulations of life, and especially the foibles of religious persons, was equal to the occasion, however, and he passed off the incident as more to the discredit of Professor Andrews than to the folly of his collaborator:

> *What, please, was your motive in submitting to Dr. Andrews the Friends in Need chapter? I might even add sternly, And with what authority did you do this? . . . He (Dr. Andrews) does not wish anyone else to touch his heroic Quakers, whom, to all appearance, he regards as his own personal property. To approach them in a spirit of levity is, I infer, to blaspheme; and in fact, it should rather dull the point of Dr. Andrews' book, when, and if, it appears.*
>
> *I have answered him with a silken civility. All the same, I trust you are not thus passing around for general inspection bits of an uncompleted book, bits which in themselves I expect to revise.*

The chapter on the Quakers was written as a first draft by Hanna and then worked and re-worked by Cabell into a masterpiece of mockery. It must have been a source of anxiety for Hanna, responsible for the historical accuracy of the book, but more or less unable to prevent Cabell from processing the facts so that they read more like the doings of Holy Holmendis (a fictional character in "The Biography") than anything known on earth. It is understandable that Hanna should have submitted his manuscript to a knowledgeable colleague. But Cabell was equally determined to write a readable book, and a saleable one, and the only way he knew how to do this was to impose on the "plot," as it were, his own strange view of things.

When once he had animated the text to his own satisfaction he was difficult to discourage and became largely impervious to criticism. On 15 August 1942 he wrote to Hanna:

> *Our Quakers and our Bartram are nicely vivid. Once get them into the market, and nobody will accept a more dull substitute. I refer you to the majestic example of Gibbon. He made his history good reading, and so the errors of which he has been convicted time and again have simply been dismissed.*

On 14 September 1942 he had misgivings about the progress of the book:

> *It is my private opinion that our book is becoming about as dull stuff as I ever read. I do not doubt that the material is of value from the point of view of history, but the slump in rascality after Kingsley leaves me appalled and drowsy. Even you, I think, are beginning to take naps while writing it: "Another noted visitor noted so-and-so," "Forts to protect the river settlements were erected at the settlements," "The capacity of the hotels was often taxed to their capacity,"&c. And I do not in the least blame you: I feel merely that we are getting into the somnolent style of the series.*

Hanna evidently took this sort of chaff in good part but one tends, on reading such criticism, to rally to his defense. He was busy on a book of his own about Murat, had just been married, and was a full-time teacher, as well as the provider of the first draft of each chapter for Mr. Cabell. The high standard of most of his writing is amply established by the inclusion in the final text of whole passages, pages, and even chapters that are substantially unchanged from his first drafts.

In a recent book on Cabell, Desmond Tarrant has called the treatment in *The St. Johns* (p. 269) of the great ornithologist and artist, J. J. Audubon, "ungenerous."[8] What is suggested there is that Audubon left the schooner provided for him in 1832 by the American government "in a tantrum" at finding nothing of interest by the St. Johns River. The true story appears to be that the ship was recalled for repairs, but the text quotes a letter Audubon wrote to his wife grumbling about the scarcity of birds in the Floridas and implies that he left the schooner in disgust. Actually, the substance of this chapter is Hanna's and he must take responsibility for both the critical tone and the historicity of the incident. What can be said is that the amusing tale of the pomposity and foibles of the great naturalist makes good reading and includes a spirited defense of Florida's richness in the rare birds that Audubon was unlucky enough to miss.

The period of the Civil War (which both Cabell and Hanna think of as the "War Between the States") receives more extensive but equally idiosyncratic treatment. We learn that the yacht "America," winner of the race around the Isle of Wight in 1851, was the most famous of the blockade runners to use the St. Johns River. We are told also of the adventure on the St. Johns in which a fugitive Confederate general, John Cabell Breckenridge, escaped to Cuba and thence to England. Cabell, with his predilection for family names, must have enjoyed putting in this story.

Harriet Beecher Stowe, in a chapter written in its entirety by Cabell, is not treated kindly:

Never at any instant during the period that she was composing Uncle Tom's Cabin, A Tale of Life Among the Lowly, had it been necessary for Mrs. Calvin Ellis Stowe to leave Brunswick, Maine, in order to explain or to describe or to denounce anything concerning the South.[9]

She falls into the terms of reference of the book by purchasing, after the end of the Civil War, a property in Florida in order to rehabilitate her alcoholic son. The whole episode is treated as fiction, with dialogue between Mrs. Stowe and her son in Cabellian comedic style. To Cabell's obvious relish the son deserts his mother, and Mrs. Stowe is left to write a series of papers on the St. Johns, which resulted "in an immediate and a most profitable increase of tourist travel from out of the North"[10] This is icy; the treatment of Menendez and Rolle was kindly in comparison. It is on such subjects that, in contrast to the usual impersonal, Gibbonian irony, the strong feelings of a Southerner obtrude and we remember that the author is "Bob Cabell's son," born not long after the end of the Civil War to the son of General Lee's personal physician.[11]

General Lee, too, visited Florida for his health, and Cabell, in amplification of a mere hint in Hanna's draft, gives a moving account of his reception on his steamer at Jacksonville:

The old hero was forced also, by the disappointed requirements of filial love and devotion, to appear on deck, so that he might at least be seen by his people. The wharves were packed with his people, and not one of them cheered now; for indeed a Southerner of this period would as soon have though of applauding God. There was, instead, a complete silence; and it was not only the women who wept.[12]

Those who criticize Cabell for having a negative attitude toward life, or toward the United States, or toward the United States, or toward the Southerners from whom he sprung, would be advised to read his account of the early life of Napoleon B. Broward, Governor of Florida (1905-9). In a postscript to his letter to Hanna of 14 September 1942, Cabell says that "with Broward I think I can do fairly well by quoting freely from the pamphlet. It seems to be a Horatio Alger story that actually did happen." However, the story of Broward is touched by Cabell's best gifts as a novelist and, in addition, it reveals a patriotic streak that he normally kept well concealed. He drops all pretence of writing formal history as he paints for us a novelist's picture of the mere ruins out of which Broward's father, a former Southern Senator, had to erect some sort of existence for his wife and family. (One is reminded of an equally distinguished treatment of this theme in the concluding portion of Benet's epic poem, *John Brown's Body*.) Under such post-cataclysmic circumstances the children of this formerly well-to-do family could hardly be educated; it was a heroic struggle to get them fed. And their situation was "far from unique," as Cabell points out:

He (Broward) came out of a log cabin beside the St. Johns, alone and unaided and but one-tenth educated, into the most lofty political stations . . . Yet this is a performance which, to us in America, has become trite . . . .
The land's work, in brief, under a democracy, is done by no genius but by the man of normal mental equipment such as was Broward; . . . that is what thousands of yet other commonplace persons have been doing, without any ostentation, and as a mere matter of course, alongside the St. Johns River, for rather more than three and half centuries.[13]

It is this note of pride in American achievement that changes the whole tone of *The St. Johns*. Perhaps it destroys its unity. The author-novelist stops playing God with his historical puppets and reveals a tragic sense as well as a sense of personal involvement in this history of his native land.

The last episode of the book, which like Broward's story was written by Cabell without a draft by Hanna, tells of the Jacksonville lady of easy virtue who became Stephen Crane's wife and shared with him his period of literary lionization in England. On Crane's death in 1900, she returned to Jacksonville and died of drink ten years later. It is a sordid tale and gives an odd, unhappy twist to the book. But there is little doubt that Cabell, having revealed so much of his heart in the penultimate chapters, desired to end on a note that Gibbon would have approved. The story leaves a bad taste, however, and shows that morbid streak which Edmund Wilson noted as one of Cabell's outstanding characteristics as a writer.[14] (Wilson observed it particularly in the two works that are set in Florida—*There Were Two Pirates* (1946) and *The Devil's Own Dear Son* (1949)—and appears not to have read *The St. Johns,* which certainly provides additional evidence of the truth of his observation.) The letters to Hanna reveal how much trouble Cabell took—or, more accurately, how much trouble he imposed on Hanna—to get the details of this episode right:

> *One needs, I am sure, a little more pictorial detail, especially as to the last years of Cora's life in Jacksonville, How was the house furnished? Did the young ladies receive, for example, in kimonos, or was etiquette more of the Emily Post order? What sort of pictures adorned the walls? Did Cora maintain her intimacy with—a delicious thought—Henry James? . . . (9 July 1942)*

The epilogue, which purports to be a dialogue between Hanna and Cabell, is in the tradition of Georgian belles-lettres. Hanna produced a straightforward prose draft of this section, but Cabell selected material and re-wrote it as a dialogue. A few loose ends are tied up; some new names are mentioned, such as Frederick Delius, who was sent to Florida at the age of twenty by his father in an attempt to frustrate his desire to be a professional musician. The dialogue expresses the cameraderie and happy collaboration of the two authors. And there the book ends.

It is clear from the correspondence that when he had completed the book approximately to his satisfaction, Cabell sent it off to the publisher, in cavalier fashion, without consulting Hanna, who had no idea of how much re-writing Cabell had done on the final text.

On 19 February 1943 Cabell informed Hanna that "the book is finished. I am surprised that he (John Farrar of Farrar and Rinehart) does not ask us staunch confederates to soften our expressions." Hanna was not at all happy about this and on 20 March expressed himself as "deeply concerned over the final form of our typescript. . . Since I am responsible for the major part of the historical content of the book I must, as all historians must, employ the utmost care in seeing that statements are accurate." Cabell replied breezily on 21 March that there was "not . . . I think, any special reason for worry over the final form of the book," and added slyly that "The diction has been much improved—though I say it—but factually I have changed nothing." He assured Hanna that all corrections had been incorporated, and mentioned, at the end of the letter, the sudden death of Benet, who had written to Cabell "on the evening of the twelfth as to his pleasure in the book, and died before daybreak."

With admirable consistency—for this was what he had said at the start—Cabell reiterated his philosophy regarding the book:

> *I still decline to consider the book as a history. It is an account of various persons who have lived beside the St. Johns; and our main use for history has been to employ it as a background which set off the traits of these persons, and even then, only during the while that they were concerned with the river. (9 April 1943)*

Cabell, as we can see, had had it his own way all the time. His collaborator had deferred to the older man as to the book's policy and had seen much of his material discarded or re-written. Those who sneer at the concept of the "Southern gentleman" should note the genuine and consistent refinement shown by both men in this correspondence—but from start to finish Cabell had dictated the book's form, had had the final say in the development of its every detail, and had established its literary type. It can be argued that this was not an orthodox history book—and Hanna, after all, was not objecting to that, but was merely anxious to avoid errors for which he, and he only would be blamed. As to real history, he would write his own.

The book, once published, had a mixed reception, but Cabell was an experience sailor on stormier seas than these. The most serious blow was struck by a certain Mr. Yonge, about whom Cabell's customary charity failed when he dealt with the attack at length in his letter to Hanna of 31 December 1943:

> Take next Mr. Yonge. . . . I resented from the beginning the notion of submitting anything I had written to his approval, but since you desired to have him pass on the text, I let that pass also. That after having, as I understand it, given his imprimatur, he should decree the history garbled and imaginary and something or other else, confirms my original opinion of him. . . . I can but regard him as an instance of the disadvantages of interbreeding between the jackass and the skunk.

He exulted, on 21 March 1944, over a rumored fourth printing, "although this, as in radio war news (apart from grumbling about shortage of gasoline, this is the only mention of the second world war in the correspondence), is not confirmed by any official source. We may yet be the best seller in the River Series." On 21 May 1944, he mentioned the favorable notice in the *American Historical Review,* which delighted but also surprised him because, as he put it, he "did not know that the Holy Ghost had ever taken up writing, and this article, while obviously done by some member of the Trinity, is not quite in the style of either the Father or of the Son."

After this first success in a historical work, Cabell was urged by his publishers to find another collaborator and to do another historical book. After having rejected a number of ideas, he had reported to Hanna on 2 February 1944 that he had "made a sort of a start upon a non-fiction book which concerns more or less remotely the state of Virginia." This was to become *Let Me Lie* (1947), which so intrigued Edmund Wilson when he read it—he had previously dismissed Cabell as a second-rate romancer—that he decided to read some of Cabell's novels, subsequently producing two articles which still rank as the most authoritative criticism Cabell has evoked.

The St. Johns seems to be in every way a better book than *Let Me Lie* and it reflects great credit on the collaborators. Cabell gave himself a great deal of work—which, if he had regarded the book as a pot-boiler, he need not have done—by looking for characters about whom he had something to say. One can only conjecture what burdens, in his insistence on discovering details which appealed to his novelist's eye, he imposed on Hanna. What is clear from the correspondence is that the men remained firm friends and were corresponding almost up to the time of Cabell's death in 1958. *The St. Johns* remains. As Cabell boasted cheerfully to Hanna on 9 April 1943, ". . . it is an extremely good book, for all that its own authors may not agree as to its nature."

NOTES

[1] James Branch Cabell, and A. J. Hanna, *The St. Johns: A Parade of Diversities,* (New York: Farrar and Rinehart, Inc., 1943).
[2] James Branch Cabell, *As I Remember It* (new York: The McBride Co., 1955), p. 208.
[3] *As I Remember It,* p. 209.
[4] Edmund Wilson, *The Bit Between My Teeth,* "The James Branch Cabell Case Re-opened" (New York: Farrar, Straus and Giroux, 1939), p. 304.
[5] *The St. Johns,* p. 35.
[6] Joe Lee Davis, *James Branch Cabell* (New York: Twayne Publications, Inc., 1962), p. 139.
[7] *The St. Johns,* p. 132.
[8] Desmond Tarrant, *James Branch Cabell* (University of Oklahoma Press, 1967), p. 268.
[9] *The St. Johns,* p. 222.
[10] *The St. Johns,* p. 233.
[11] James Branch Cabell, *Let Me Lie* (New York: Farrar, Straus, and Giroux, 1947), p. 164.
[12] *The St. Johns,* p. 240-241.
[13] *The St. Johns,* p. 260-261.
[14] Edmund Wilson, *The Bit Between My Teeth,* p. 323.

SINCLAIR LEWIS AND HIS ATTEMPTS TO REFORM JAMES BRANCH CABELL

In the author's note to the Storisende edition of *The Cream of the Jest,* Cabell tells the story, rather obliquely, of the rejection of his book, then entitled *In the Flesh,* by Sinclair Lewis. Lewis was at the time a publisher's reader for George H. Doran Company and his letter, dated February 15, 1915, is not at all the usual polite letter of rejection; it is a heartfelt, swingeing attack on Cabell's attitude to life.[1] "I do not believe this book lives," he writes, "I do not believe it is, indeed, in the flesh. The phrase 'midnight oil' keeps coming back to me as I read it. And there is another phrase which comes back to me. It is this: 'Sore on the world.' Are you?"

The two men eventually met and became friends. They kept up a desultory correspondence over many years, but by far the most interesting item in their exchanges was this initial, very sincere, basically kindly assault by Lewis on Cabell's work. It would seem that he misunderstood what Cabell was getting at in the book and it is not surprising that Cabell did not bother sustantially to revise it, contenting himself with submitting the manuscript no less than seven times to different publishers between 1915 and 1917 before having it accepted by McBride's on the second time around.

The central portion of the letter is a reasoned plea to Cabell to stop insulting the very people—that is, the publishers—on whom his living depends. The passage is worth quoting in its entirety.

> *And I shall probably delight your soul—proving the kinship of all publishers—by saying that the letters on pages 46 and 7, and the burlesque upon the following pages, first amused me, then pleased my sense of ingenuity, but ended by leaving a very bad taste in my mouth. Do you really suppose that any publisher in the country is going to offer such an insult to Dodd, Mead and Company as to publish a book in which they are referred to as "Dead, Mudd and Company?" To say nothing of the insult to my very good friends of the Century Company implied in referring to that company as "The Cemetery Company?" Doubtless if I preferred those firms to my own, I should make an endeavor to be with them instead of with Doran. But the fact that I prefer my own firm does not at all indicate that I have any desire to insult them publicly and unpleasantly: and I should most certainly regard it as a direct affront to them to countenance the publication of a book in which they were referred to as they are in these pages of yours. Nor does the fact that I have loved the sheer beauty of some of your stories, keep me from resenting your reference to Mrs. Wharton's "The Customs of the Country", as "The Cuspidors of the Countryman." This despite the fact that your variation of her name as "Mrs. Seeketh Haut-Ton" is most charmingly ingenious.*
>
> *Finally I seriously doubt whether any one who is not closely connected with the world of book-minding would be in the least amused by these pages.*

This is a little pompous and professorial—"I should most certainly regard it as a direct affront to them to countenance . . ."—and Lewis is aware that his "sermon", as he calls it, is directed by a younger man of even less literary eminence than the recipient. Cabell was thirty-six and had published by this date five "not very marketable" (Cabell's phrase) novels. Lewis was thirty-one and the work for which he is renowned was all ahead of him. He had, however, made a tentative start as an author with *Our Mr. Wren* (1914). His second novel, *The Trail of the Hawk* was to be published in 1915.

Lewis was right, of course, about the necessity to avoid gratuitous insults to publishers and high literary personages — though Cabell's sallies retain their ability to make us laugh. In the 1917 version of the novel the discussion of publishers and authors, which Lewis had objected to, was omitted. When Cabell revised the novel for publication in 1922, however, he put back the chapter entitled "Of Publishing," but "Dead, Mudd and Company" and "The Cemetery Company" no longer appear. The offending publishers are now "Dapley and Pildriff," "The Baxon-Muir Company" and "Leeds, McKibble and Todd." But this was after the notorious *Jurgen* case and Cabell has added to his original chapter some passages that obviously refer obliquely to the suppression of that book and, ironically, to the useful publicity it gave to the author's work.

Lewis's main point in his long letter is that since Cabell "can do beautiful things in a country which is not overrun with beauty, we cannot afford to have you 'Sore on the world.'[1] *The Cream of the Jest*, however, is not, in essence, a depressing tale. The Sigil of Scoteia, a magical device which enables Felix Kenneston to carry out a Cook's tour of the ages in search of Ettarre — it is one of the major symbols in the book — turns out to be the broken metal top of Mrs. Kenneston's cold-cream jar. Here we are at the heart of the Cabellian experience. On the face of it the message is one of disillusionment — the falling back from the quest for ideal beauty and perfect love, which Ettarre represents — but alongside the disillusion is the affirmation of purely human values which, against the backdrop of the dreams, strike us with great force. Kenneston, in the light of his experiences in the world of the Sigil, is overwhelmed by his feeling of ordinary human love for his fallible, uncomprehending wife, seeing that "for each and all of us the dream-haze merges into the glare of common day; the *dea certe*, whom that roseate fled light transfigured, stands confessed a simple loving woman, a creature of like flesh and limitations as our own: but who are we to mate with goddesses."[2] This may be a humble moral but no one could call it lacking in good cheer. It is hardly "Sore on the world."

It may be recalled that Edmund Wilson, in "The James Branch Cabell Case Reopened" had the impression that *The High Place* and *Something About Eve* were about damnation and he thought that the first syllable of Mispec Moor suggested hatefulness.[3] This is the same sort of misinterpretation as Sinclair Lewis's. Cabell afterwards informed Wilson that Mispec Moor was an anagram for compromise, but Wilson continued to feel that the effect on the reader was "Not at all such as the author says he intends."

We know from Cabell's autobiographical works that he was a happy man and that his domestic circumstances were satisfactory, rather than otherwise, and it is clear that he defended himself from Lewis's charge because, in a second letter with the letterhead of George H. Doran Company, dated February 15, 1915, Lewis says "I am glad indeed to learn from your letter that life is brighter than, from your novel, I had judged it to be. In that case, all my remarks on your novel may be reduced to the statement that it did not 'get me'—"

Twelve years later, in a letter dated February 14, 1927 and with the letterhead of a hotel in St. James Square, Sinclair Lewis once again writes a very long letter to his friend — and once again urges him to action.

> *I don't know that I have very definitely "got anything out of" almost a year in Europe — out of trattorie in Roma, a half-timbered cottage in Kent, crush teas at Lady Colefax's in London — except the important thing of having enjoyed myself. I remain, I suppose, (perhaps to my advantage) incurably a brisk and provincial American. It's not at all that I prefer Americanism, or advocate it; I simply am it. I could be happy in Europe the rest of my life; in a year I could be speaking at least a comprehensible Italian, and altogether happy in a villa at — oh, perhaps Rapallo, or on Lake Garda. But throughout I remain cheerfully conscious of Midwestern woodboxes and wheat-shocks, of New York elevateds, of the travelling salesman with whom I feel so natural.*

> But why – in – hell you, who are of essence European, whom I can so beautifully see in a vettura (and in an eye-glass) on the Pincio, or on the Place Vendome, or on Piccadilly – why you should remain in America is beyond me. Hugh and I (Hugh Walpole) quite arranged it the other evening. We have a Tudor cottage for you– a neat little place with twenty bedrooms – and a rose garden and a library collected for ten generations, and the whole damned thing costs what a two-rooms-and-bath does in America, and the neighborhood baroness (beer by origin but books by quite real instinct) comes round and begs you to come to tea, and you have much more fun not going than you have out of not going places in Richmond!

It is, perhaps, not extraordinary that Sinclair Lewis should have difficulty in understanding his friend, for it is Cabell's Southern-ness that he could not grasp. Cabell certainly did not respond to Lewis's letter by rushing off to England to enjoy crush teas at Lady Colefax's or live in a Tudor cottage near a baroness. He stayed in Richmond, Virginia and wrote books which, as Wilson pointed out admiringly, became more and more "perversely unpublishable."[4] A Southerner of the "old stock," as Cabell described himself, had one great advantage and one great disability, when compared to his fellow Americans to the north and west. He had no identity problem; and he came from a defeated people. The fact that he knew exactly who he was and who his great-great-grandfather was, is an advantage that not many of us possess. It does not make Cabell one bit less American than Lewis, but it substantially reduced the lure of Lady Colefax's teas. That he came from people who were once rich and secure and who had been reduced by a cataclysmic civil conflict to something like hardship was a disadvantage that affected his whole outlook on life. This is something that is common to many Southern writers and it accounts for the tragic note in so much Southern literature. In Cabell's hands, though, the note of "vanity of vanities, all is vanity" does not have the harsh reverberation of personal bitterness. His view of human history, though, was cynical in the extreme and he did not subscribe to the idea that everthing that has taken place in America over the centuries had been divinely guided to turn out for the best.

In *The St. Johns,* a book he wrote with A. J. Hanna for the Rivers of America Series, nothing was more evident than the attitude of humourous dismay at human folly that possessed the joint authors, both of whom were Southerners of the same ilk. It is impossible to tell, for instance, in the published text, where Hanna's writing ends and Cabell's commences because they are both possessed by the same corrosive cynicism with regard to human motives. But none of this is personally felt bitterness; it is a heritage; they can be quite cheerful themselves while they make the reader squirm in his chair.

The literary expression of this sensibility, however, has been widely misunderstood. *The St. Johns* was a scandal to many who did not see the jokes; and many less sophisticated Southerners did not see that the picture Cabell and Hanna presented was central to the feeling about history that they themselves, as Southerners, shared. It is hardly surprising that both Edmund Wilson and Sinclair Lewis, trying to come to terms with Cabell's novels, were led to the conclusion that his message was morbid and frightening, and, in Lewis's case, that his life was a sad one. It is amusing to note, on both occassions, Cabell's firm but courteous disclaimer.

NOTES

[1] Alderman Library, University of Virginia, 7777-1, 1915-1913.
[2] James Branch Cabell, *The Cream of the Jest,* Storisewde Edition, p. 226.
[3] Edmund Wilson, *The Bit Between My Teeth,* New York, Farrar, Straus & Giroux, 1939, p.315.
[4] Edmund Wilson, p. 303.

CABELL UNDER FIRE

In the 1920's James Branch Cabell never seemed to lack friends or enemies. Some of his friends, indeed, doubled for enemies, like H. L. Mencken and Louis Untermeyer. The English were, as they still are, generally more favourable towards him than his own countrymen. Though J. C. Squire attacked him in "The London Mercury," Hugh Walpole remained an unwavering propagandist of his talents. Cabell, however, had a bad time of it as well as a good time of it throughout the decade. He had the satisfaction of seeing the publication, in 1927, of the eighteen-volume Storisende Edition of *The Works of James Branch Cabell,* but he had the constant disappointment of having his subsequent works compared unfavourably with his 1919 *succes de scandale, Jurgen.* A good example of his demeanour under fire is shown in his reply to hostile criticism of *Figures of Earth* (1921) — while *Jurgen* was still under ban — from a particularly sensitive quarter.

In "The Literary Review" of April 23, 1921, published by the New York Evening Post, Maurice Hewlett sharply attacked Cabell's new novel. His view is substantially intended to be an expose of Cabell's ignorance of medieval lore and, by contrast, Hewlett's own better understanding of the matter. It is written with a total lack of humour, and although intended to exploit Cabell's weakness it only succeeds in revealing his strength.

To understand the situation we have to understand something about Maurice Hewlett. Born in 1861 at Weybridge, Kent — and therefore fifty-nine years of age in 1921— he had, in spite of strong literary proclivities, been trained as a lawyer and had taken over from his father as Keeper of Land Revenue Records. His interest in antiquarian law was, therefore, professional and extensive. He was more of a scholar than anything else, though he had wished above all to be recognized as a poet and had received some recognition for his long poem, *Song of the Plow.* His medieval romance, *Forest Lovers* (1898), was a best-seller and had brought him before a wide public, but his gifts as a novelist were slight in comparison with Cabell's. Unsupported by a strong, historical plot-line, he tended to overload his works with elaborate settings. *The Queen's Quair,* (1904), a novel about Mary Queen of Scots, was successful because his historical imagination, supported by a sound knowledge of the period, was adequate for a novel based on history. And he had the same sort of success with his account of Coeur de Lion and the Crusades in *The Life and Death of Richard Yea-and-Nay,* (1900). His originality in *Forest Lovers* is largely a matter of reproducing the effects of Malory's prose style, a series of literary tricks that Cabell seems to have acquired for himself without much compunction.

Cabell had been a warm admirer of Hewlett for twenty years, bought all his books as soon as they were published and recommended them enthusiastically to his friends. As Paul Spencer [1] has pointed out in his interesting discussion of Cabell's literary relationship to Hewlett, the younger man borrowed, in addition to some points of style, the device of invented authorities, the subtitling of novels as "Comedies," and the practice of ending each book with the medieval form "Explicit." Cabell's early novels, such as *Chivalry* (1909) and *The Soul of Melicent* (1913), are very close in subject and treatment to Hewlett's romances, but by 1921 he had already drawn away from his youthful fascination with merely romantic happenings in never-never-lands and was beginning to use a hodge-podge of archaic and invented material to express a highly individual and delicately humourous philosophy of life. Essentially, it is Cabell's criticism of life that gives to his work a dimension that separates it from that of Hewlett and puts him more properly in the company of Swift and Anatole France.

The situation between these two authors was complicated by the fact that Hewlett had outlived his earlier popularity, whereas Cabell was at this time, for however short a period, a celebrity. The suppression of *Jurgen* on January 14, 1920, and the seizing of copies of the book from his publishers, had made him instantly a notorious writer whose next book was awaited with eagerness in the hope that it would contain ever more prurient material than *Jurgen*. *Figures of Earth* was to be a disappointment, in this respect, to public and critic alike, but meanwhile the trial of *Jurgen* pended and was not to begin until October 16, 1922. It is clear that Hewlett had some understandable motives for wishing to question Cabell's work, and it would be interesting to know whether the New York Post solicited the review or whether Hewlett volunteered it. If the suggestion came from Hewlett we could be more certain of his personal sense of grievance towards Cabell. As it is we can only suggest that there is, from internal evidence, an animus more personal than literary in Hewlett's approach.

Literary quarrels can be as distressing as quarrels within a family. Indeed, they are often rather like family quarrels because writers so often stand in a familial relationship to one another. When H. G. Wells turned his critical eye towards his friend Henry James, James responded as if he were dealing with a disloyal younger brother. Similarly, Maurice Hewlett seems to have been outraged, not only at Cabell's success in his own genre, but at his daring to do something different from Maurice Hewlett. He seems to have taken it for granted that Cabell was a romancer like himself, trying to use detail from a past age in a scholarly manner to give colour to a tale. His review of *Figures of Earth,* however, studiously avoided mention of any real literary debts that Cabell may have owed to himself. Mrs. James Branch Cabell, in conversation with this writer, said that Cabell would have cheerfully acknowledged such debts, but when Hewlett questioned his learning and his good taste he had no alternative but to reply in kind.

The article was insultingly entitled "The Essentials of Nonsense" and Hewlett began by quoting Charles II's remark about a court preacher that "his nonsense suited other people's nonsense." He then accused Cabell of pretended learning, of taking "a clout" of Rabelais, "a pinch" of Anatole France, but of serving up this mixture with little regard for its fitness.

The main thrust of his criticism was that Cabell was so ill-educated that he did not understand the rules that must govern the use of historical material.

> *Mr. Cabell's acquaintance with medieval lore seems to be mainly with names. Skillfully used, as M. France uses them, they will take you far, for they have within them their own magic. Provence will give you a picture, a perfume, an air. Print the name Raymond Berenger and it will work if you let it. Names are symbols, as all words are. But if you mishandle them, through ignorance or coxcombery, or wantonness, or mere frivolity, they will do nothing for you; used as Mr. Cabell uses them they cancel out like fractions in a sum.*

The least offensive explanation he gave for Cabell's use of names was that of frivolity, but he clearly meant to accuse him of ignorance, not only of "medieval lore" but of geography.

> *His hero, Manuel, who though he has a Byzantine name, must be assumed Scandinavian of sorts, goes from Norway, let us say, to Albania, where he becomes acquainted with Helmas, King of that country. He then crosses the Bay of Biscay in order to reach Provence from Albania.*

After complaining that Cabell used the form "Meregrette" for Eleanor of Aquitaine's daughter, Margaret, he pointed out the absurdity of a war which seemed to involve Ferdinand of Navarre (sic), Cordova, the Catalans and the Philistines. It did not seem to occur to him that Cabell did this sort of thing deliberately; that he knew very well that the Philistines did not fit in the context of medieval Europe and that he expected the reader to see this. The assumption made is that Cabell did not know what he was doing; and he confused names and periods and geography because he was an ignoramus and a charlatan to boot.

A glance at Hewlett's essays and journalistic writings clearly shows that he had wide interests and was of a scholarly turn of mind. He was perhaps more learned that Cabell whose only use for learning was to fuel his creative fires. But his attack was careless and unscholarly for all that. It is not difficult to see how one can sail from Albania to Provence via the Bay of Biscay. This does not have to be Cabellian ignorance, nor even a Cabellian joke; it is the Atlantic route and might have been undertaken to avoid pirates or hostile navies. Cabell, as we shall see, had a more cogent explanation. In similar fashion, Hewlett's objection to the word "geas" backfires.

I have not the heart to go on. If I had I would ask him what a "geas" is. He makes great play with the word until he gets tired of it, using it in the sense of a spell. If it is his own invention it does not pull its weight. I know something myself about the thirteenth century, but not that word.

"Geas" turns out to be tenth century Irish and was used correctly by Cabell, as Louis Untermeyer quickly pointed out, reinforcing Cabell's own protest.

Hewlett's final sally was on the subject of what he called Cabell's "nonsense," which he judged to be not significant and "feeble" in its effect. He quoted two passages from *Figures of Earth*. The first was the mimic utterance with which Queen Freydis dismissed her frightful and ghostly retinue, before becoming fully human — "A penny, a penny, twopence, a penny and a half and a halfpenny." (Chapter XIV). He considered this to be inadequate to the occasion. The second passage concerns the congregation of birds, called up by the magic of Asparasas, to enunciate, not ultimate wisdom, but worn-out truisms like "contentment is the greatest happiness." (Chapter XI). We have seen Cabell at this game before. Both the God of Jurgen's grandmother and Koschei the Deathless, purveyed similar stale fare to Jurgen. It is one of Cabell's recurring themes that pompous oracles, when pressed to divulge their innermost secrets, tell us that two and two makes four. Hewlett, however, would neither see the joke nor take Cabell seriously enough to check his sources. He judged Cabell to be *"pedantic without science,"* but he turned out to be wrong once more.

In the April 30th edition of the Literary Review of the New York Post, Cabell replied briefly but with spirit.

To the Editor of The Literary Review:

Sir: The paper headed "The Essentials of Nonsense," by Maurice Hewlett, has a very nicely descriptive title, but as a review of my book it leaves me oddly dissatisfied. It is not merely that I can read between the lines, as it were, that Mr. Hewlett found little to enjoy in "Figures of Earth." What troubles me is that his indignant brayings partake rather of such personal idiocy as ought to be restrained in anybody who was formerly an ornament of English letters.

To the more or less crushing charge that in Manuel's dream chronology geography and nomenclature are jumbled (as in most medieval legends) the one possible reply must be, "Of course they are." To like or dislike such a mode is optional; and while such frenzied objection to it would come with a queer grace from the author of "The Forest Lovers" and "Lore of Proserpine," it comes, like any other balderdash, naturally enough from the concocter of "The Little Iliad" and "Love and Lucy." There is, thus far in Mr. Hewlett's spasms, no cause for special astonishment.

With real astonishment, however, one gathers that Mr. Hewlett is not sufficiently acquainted with the familiar story of Melusine to know that the Albania over which King Helmas reigned was in Scotland; that he is not aware St. Ferdinand was King of Castile and Leon; that his knowledge of Gaelic legend does not extend to the very common word "geas," or the famous fairy song "Pighin, pighin, da–phighin, pighin go ieith agus leith phighin," and that he is even ignorant of the cries which the Talmudic stories about Solomon ascribed to the various birds.

Still, it is not fair that I should profit by Mr. Hewlett's lack of such elementary erudition. Plain honesty compels me thus publicly and modestly to admit that when Mr. Hewlett accredits to me that invention of (and blame for) all these, and other, matters he honors me beyond my due. And while these deficiencies in Mr. Hewlett's knowledge are interesting, why, after all, should his naive confession of them be printed as a review of a book written by somebody who does happen to know about these things?
       Your faithfully, JAMES BRANCH CABELL

One of Cabell's fascinations is that he plays tricks on the general reader that only the researcher discovers. His books are full of traps for the unwary, and Hewlett overconfidently stumbled into a minefield. What must have seemed to be, at best, an ironical invention turned out to be a quotation from the Talmud. King Helmas' realm is in Scotland. "A penny, a penny" is translated from an Irish fairy song. What next? Even the reader of *Kalki,* who knows that he can never be sure when Cabell's mock-learning will turn our to be real learning, will be surprised to see the urbane mask drop, at the end of his letter, as he squarely faced the attack on his erudition and proclaimed himself "somebody who does happen to know about those things."

It is noteworthy that Cabell did not defend himself on all counts. Hewlett objected to two names—"The Prince de Gatanais, which sounds as if it might come from Saint-Simon, and the Marquess di Paz — a truly remarkable name, composed in no less than three languages." Perhaps he would have been grateful for help provided by John Cranwell and James Cover, who have told us that Paz is a common Spanish name and that there was a Prince of Paz who flourished during the eighteenth-century.[2] There does, however, seem to have been a deliberate mixture of languages, for the title is either French, or a courtesy title for the son of an English duke, and the "Di" is Portuguese. He could have defended "Prince de Gatinais," for the same authority informs us that Gatinais was a section of France in the Province of Orleans.

The matter did not end with Cabell's reply to Hewlett in the New York Evening Post. In February, 1921, the first edition of a bi-monthly literary magazine, *The Reviewer,* was published in Richmond, Virginia. Morally supported by Cabell—and for a short time guest-edited by him — the review represented a response to H. L. Mencken's jibe that the South was culturally sterile. Its editorial offices were at the residence of Margaret Waller Freeman, who was one of the youthful founders of the paper and who was later to become the second Mrs. James Branch Cabell. It received support and literary contributions from H. L. Mencken, Ellen Glasgow, John Galsworthy, Ann Lowell, Burton Bascoe, Joseph Hergesheimer, Carl Van Vechten, Louis Untermeyer and other distinguished personages.

Louis Untermeyer was the first to reinforce Cabell's reply to Hewlett in an article titled, "Hark, From the Tomb," in the May 21, 1921, issue of the paper. He made the point that Hewlett's review of *Figures of Earth,* was bad-tempered and caused by jealousy of Cabell's success, "as if the author of that once popular medieval reconstruction, *The Forest Lovers,* had seen someone poaching . . ." After a defence of Cabell's use of "geas," previously referred to, his main point seemed to be that Hewlett had missed the allegorical intentions of *Figures of Earth,* and that it was but one-third of a "tapestry" dealing with adventures of the mind *(The Cream of the Jest),* the flesh *(Jurgen),* and the spirit *(Figures of Earth).* Where Untermeyer got this last notion is not clear—perhaps from Cabell himself—but it is certainly far-fetched, and it is possible that Cabell was pulling Mr. Untermeyer's leg. In the forward to the Storisende Edition of *Figures of Earth,* Cabell tells how the germ of the idea for a book came to him as he watched his wife and child through the window of his study and had thought that they might be an illusion, part of the windows which, when opened, would show only "a grey nothingness"—a characteristic product of Cabell's dark imagination.[3] There seems to be no evidence, apart from Untermeyer's assertion, that Cabell had written a trilogy. In the order of "The Biography," *Figures of Earth* is number two, *Jurgen* is number six, and *The Cream of the Jest* is number sixteen. Additionally, the respective forwards to the books do not support any close connection between them. Untermeyer did, however, point out, for the first time, some of the rhymes and rhythms hidden in the apparent prose, a subject that has now been exhaustively covered by Warren A. McNeill.[4]

This was a particularly difficult period for Cabell. Few critics were enthusiastic over *Figures of Earth* and it was compared unfavorably with *Jurgen.* He had dedicated Book II and Book III of the novel to Untermeyer and Mencken respectively, but neither of them liked it as well as *Jurgen* and they publicly said so. He noted bitterly in his preface to the Storisende Edition that "Not many other volumes . . . have been burlesqued and cried down in public print by their own dedicatees."[5] It inspired him to write, not for the last time, his mock literary obituary.

In the next issue of *The Reviewer,* June 1, 1921, Cabell, having made his personal reply to Hewlett, answered his critics at large in an article entitled, "Exit." Quoting from the New York Globe, which had predicted a collapse of the "Cabell balloon," he referred to attacks on *Figures of Earth* by J. C. Squire, Richard Le Gallienne and Maurice Hewlett, calling them "British battlers for nineteenth century traditions," which somehow sounds like Mencken in full cry rather than Cabell. The piece is divided into three sections and each section ends with a refrain like a ballade.

> *Well, I shall be, in some ways, rather sorry to see this Cabell pass to oblivion. For I foresee that he will pass quickly now. He was nourished, he was bred and fattened and sustained, entirely upon newspaper paragraphs; and our literary editors retain a naive faith in anything, except, of course, the pound sterling, which emanates from England . . . Most of the reviewers, I fancy, are sufficiently like me to have grown a little tired of so much tall talk about Cabell, and to think it high time the monotony was varied. So this Cabell, too, must pass, with all the other novelists who have had their brief hour of being "talked about;" and this Cabell, too, must presently be at one with Marie Corelli and Maurice Hewlett and Elinor Glyn and Richard Le Gallienne and Mrs. Harriet Beecher Stowe.*

He made the point humourously enough, but he clearly showed how exasperated he was by criticism of his work based on crass comparison with *Jurgen.* "The artist," he wrote, "really must—though there is no explaining it—work either at just what he chooses or else towards exhaustion as an artist." He did not mention his American critics by name, and a casual reader might consider it to be a reply to British critics only. It is obvious, however, from the Storisende Author's Note, that he cared little for the opinion of literary men overseas and was far more concerned about the disloyalty of his American friends, chiefly Untermeyer and Mencken. It was bitter for Cabell to realize that he was more valued as a weapon against Comstockery than he was as a literary artist, and that those who applauded Jurgen's lechery were "enraged by Manuel's lack of it."[6]

Maurice Hewlett does not seem to have made any further contribution to the debate on Cabell's literary worth. Two years later he was dead. This was the beginning for Cabell of what turned out to be a permanent condition. He remained "the author of *Jurgen*" for the rest of his days and was still wryly commenting on the fact in his last autobiographical works.

NOTES

[1] *Kalki,* Vol. III, No. 4, Studies in James Branch Cabell, University of Cincinnati.
[2] Kalki, Vol. III, No. 1.
[3] James Branch Cabell, *Figures of Earth,* Storisende Edition, p. x.
[4] Kalki, Vol IV. No. 3 and subsequent issues.
[5] *Figures of Earth,* Storisende Edition, p.xv.
[6] *Figures of Earth,* Storisende Edition, p.xv.